THE
BLUE HILL

Also by Geoffrey O'Brien

POETRY

A Book of Maps
The Hudson Mystery
Floating City: Selected Poems 1978–1995
A View of Buildings and Water
Red Sky Café
Early Autumn
In a Mist

PROSE

Hardboiled America: Lurid Paperbacks and the Masters of Noir
Dream Time: Chapters from the Sixties
The Phantom Empire
The Times Square Story
Bardic Deadlines: Reviewing Poetry 1984–95
The Browser's Ecstasy: A Meditation on Reading
*Castaways of the Image Planet: Movies, Show Business, Public
    Spectacle*
Sonata for Jukebox: An Autobiography of My Ears
The Fall of the House of Walworth
Stolen Glimpses, Captive Shadows: Writing on Film 2002–2012

THE
BLUE HILL

Geoffrey O'Brien

MARSH HAWK PRESS
East Rockaway, New York • 2017

First Edition
2 4 6 8 9 7 5 3 1

Book design: Susan Quasha
Cover art: Devin Dougherty

Marsh Hawk Press books are published by Marsh Hawk Press, Inc., a not-for-profit corporation under section 501(c)3 United States Internal Revenue Code

Library of Congress Cataloging-in-Publication Data

Names: O'Brien, Geoffrey, 1948- author.
Title: The blue hill / Geoffrey O'Brien.
Description: First edition. | East Rockaway : Marsh Hawk Press, 2017.
Identifiers: LCCN 2017030931 | ISBN 9780996991100 (pbk.)
Classification: LCC PS3565.B6689 A6 2017 | DDC 811/.54—dc23 LC
record available at https://lccn.loc.gov/2017030931

Marsh Hawk Press
P.O. Box 206
East Rockaway, New York 11518-0206
www.marshhawkpress.org

For Nicholas Christopher

CONTENTS

I

The Blue Hill

1

The blue hill
Who is there who

The blue hill
Who is in with who
Who is after who

The blue hill
Who is it hides
Who is it hoots
Who is it harrows

The blue hill
Who called to who
Down the hollow

The blue hill
Who there is who

2

The blue hill
Some have been there

The blue hill
The eyes are changed
The voice is altered

The blue hill
When two that have gone there
Meet by chance
They nod their heads

The blue hill
A nod that nobody
Else gets sight of

The blue hill
Who ever dreamt of such a place

3

The blue hill
So many have been there

The blue hill
They burn to go back
They are thirsty to go back

The blue hill
Once they have been there
They walk unseen
Among their neighbors

The blue hill
They have traveled in the dark
And brought the dark back

The blue hill
Is all the time more crowded

4

The blue hill
Knock on air

The blue hill
Knock on sod
Knock on rock

The blue hill
Those who visit it
Gain hidden names
And learn the unspoken tongue

The blue hill
Everything glistens there
Everything has power there

The blue hill
Has entrances others can't see

5

The blue hill
Flickers ever in twilight

The blue hill
So marvelous
The bodies can fly there

The blue hill
When the fires
Are set blazing
Such songs come

The blue hill
Has inner walls
That shimmy like gems

The blue hill
The noise knocks the smoke open

6

The blue hill
Blue is not even blue there

The blue hill
Red is not red
Water not water even

The blue hill
What herbs grow
What round dances
Start in the dark there

The blue hill
The pitch of the music
Tears at their seams

The blue hill
They slip out of their skin like serpents

7

The blue hill
The ancient cave

The blue hill
Where bodies lock
Into a blind groove

The blue hill
Where surrounded
By nothing but terror
They cling to the pivot point

The blue hill
Where they are all
That holds the dark back

The blue hill
The smoldering hill

8

The blue hill
Babbles like a baby

The blue hill
Flips its thralls
And flaps them

The blue hill
Plucks its flasks
Whips out the wheels
And pops

The blue hill
Flickers its folds
And combs them

The blue hill
Goes up the down way

9

The blue hill
Whose blue is toxic

The blue hill
Whose blue is like a wound
Whose blue is like a swamp

The blue hill
Whose blue is like rock splotch
Whose blue is like pond scum
Whose blue is like snake froth

The blue hill
Whose blue has swollen
In every nerve path

The blue hill
Whose blue is swallowed flame

10

The blue hill
Who has not gone there

The blue hill
Some come back smiling
Like lovers after love

The blue hill
Some found the door shut
And come back groaning
Like felons after punishment

The blue hill
All who are bidden
Must go

The blue hill
Latecomers must suffer

11

The blue hill
It's a thing

The blue hill
Can't remember
Where'd I hear that

The blue hill
Some were wise to it
But who knows who
First spread the word

The blue hill
By now everybody
Has that sound in the head

The blue hill
Hear how it hums

12

The blue hill
Slides off the tongue

The blue hill
A name they caught hold of
And had to keep repeating

The blue hill
Stakes out
The far edge
Of the medicine patch

The blue hill
Beyond that
It's forbidden to be stranded

The blue hill
Is a trembling

13

The blue hill
Everybody talking about

The blue hill
Cows fell down dead
And every blister festered

The blue hill
The sky broke in pieces
The plantings were smashed
By hailstones

The blue hill
Nothing is the same
After a thing like that

The blue hill
The accursed hill

14

The blue hill
A proofless allegation

The blue hill
A vacant phrase
Mumbled by farm hands

The blue hill
Lately the source
Of complaints too rough
To be sidelined

The blue hill
Folklore is a bloody mess
Theology is like fine crystal

The blue hill
A matter to be sorted out

15

The blue hill
Boys know who went there

The blue hill
Gifted children
Can tell by looking

The blue hill
They are brought to a settlement
And point a finger
At people they never met

The blue hill
Bailiffs transport the boys
House them in pens

The blue hill
It is terrifying to be looked at

16

The blue hill
How can they tell about it

The blue hill
Believe the children
Taken where they didn't want to go

The blue hill
With eyes forced to stay open
They saw the way faces changed
They would know them anywhere

The blue hill
They came back maimed
They came back clean

The blue hill
The children are the conduit

17

The blue hill
I don't know a thing about it

The blue hill
I don't know who you are
Or what language you speak in

The blue hill
I was walking in the sunlight
Of a wide hall
My thoughts wide like the hall

The blue hill
When my breath
Was interrupted

The blue hill
I'm handled like a hauled bale

18

The blue hill
Who at last are you

The blue hill
Who can I be
Once you began to speak

The blue hill
I know the lustful eye
And now know the instant
When it sours to blood lust

The blue hill
What can I yield
That is not already taken

The blue hill
At this place I was lost

19

The blue hill
It is frightful to suffer

The blue hill
Who soak up too much pain
May fall in despair

The blue hill
It is terrible to be burned while alive
Better to be strangled
Before the body is thrown on the fire

The blue hill
Holier to allow
The mercy of the quick kill

The blue hill
Is purified by silence

20

The blue hill
That souls not be killed

The blue hill
To rack them
But not kill their souls

The blue hill
Bind them
And bring them toward the fire
But not kill their souls

The blue hill
To stifle their breath
In prayer

The blue hill
To save all souls

21

The blue hill
Where the gone went

The blue hill
The blood hill
The blear hill

The blue hill
The empty rock
A prisoner
Broke a fist on

The blue hill
The stoved hearth
The raked-over yard

The blue hill
The chilled wall

22

The blue hill
Sold at the going rate

The blue hill
What is it worth
To keep on being

The blue hill
A transfer of assets
Whether in landed property
Or gold or fine cloth

The blue hill
To name the price
Of not being named

The blue hill
Stripped for ransom

23

The blue hill
No longer believed in

The blue hill
Hangs in the air
Like a hole where cloth was

The blue hill
The soil still reeks
The smear of ashes
Sticks to the fingers

The blue hill
The color of its absence
Grips the horizon

The blue hill
Never believed in

24

The blue hill
Never was

The blue hill
Has been scorched
Out of memory

The blue hill
The boys who demanded money
Confessed their extortion
And were dragged off by their trainers

The blue hill
The burnt bones of those who went there
Are scattered in coastal towns

The blue hill
The unmarked grave

25

The blue hill
The blue heath

The blue hill
The blue cliff
The blue cleft

The blue hill
The blue claw
The blue cone
The blue stain

The blue hill
The blue shelf
The blue sheath

The blue hill
The blue

II

Excerpt from a History

"Cet arbre est sorti de sa place" (Théophile de Viau)

There have been letters of flame by night
and there have been black winds by day.

Streams have run backwards.
Boulders have risen and walked.

A leaf has returned to the tree
and a flower to the stem.

Men have drunk brine,
have fed on rock and slept in snow.

A swallow spoke. A statue sang
and its hand, lifted in benediction, bled.

A priest ran naked, a soldier wept,
a child came bearded from the womb.

The towns are hushed. From the hills come cries
and in deserts the ancient dead go wandering.

Bonfires out of ash have sprung;
a rain of blood has fallen on the plain.

Public Notice

To have entered these premises
is regarded as tantamount
to a voluntary agreement

to be photographed or searched
or to provide upon request
evidence of personal identity

the possession of a name being
considered sufficient indication
of existence as to render said possessor

subject to verbal description
or photographic recording
for any aim or purpose

contingent on such existence
as may be construed to warrant access
to a space herewith recognized

as distinct from any previous point of ingress
in being regulated by zoning
that may obligate the systematic coordination

of all relevant authenticating traits
such that to loiter within the perimeter
of any area so demarcated

is to make applicable
the pre-emptive encryption
of peripheral attributes

or encumbrances
either concealed
or openly displayed

by way of acknowledgment
that the persistence of such a barrier
renders mandatory the resolution

of any disputed claim whether tendered
or liable to be tendered
in any future eventuality

further establishing that such claim
in the presence of authorized personnel
in a context yet to be determined

will be interpreted as acquiescence
in the distribution and implementation
of any potential alternative proposition

on the part of any such properly designated agent
under which circumstance the person or persons
held to have willfully or with malicious intent

disregarded such designation
may be deemed peremptorily
and for all subsequent purposes

as unregistered
and in consequence
not yet validated.

Full Disclosure

Because I say so
is why this is true.

Why should I lie.
Why should anyone

lie about having become
unable to say anything

but what the heart urges –
a condition so rare

there is no name for it yet
even if it is already

an object of study
at a secure location

whose coordinates cannot be made public
without jeopardizing those specialists

who have sacrificed
their own freedom of agency

to ensure the ongoing viability
of that instinctive and unquestioning trust

on which each of us depends
for a working definition of truth.

Restaurant Rating

Since in this restaurant pleasure
is the appetizer and suffering

the main course, some try
to beat the system by ordering

two or three appetizers in lieu
of entree (even if the bill

comes more or less to the same);
as for dessert, if you're lucky,

it's a few moments of relative calm
before they boot you out

to clear the table for the customers
waiting impatiently by the door;

for some the accompanying drinks
really make the experience, some indeed

would rather drink than eat,
and many customers agree that

the talk before and between the courses
is what dining here is finally about;

a bit pricey, but not a bad bet;
and at any rate in this notoriously

under-served neighborhood
it doesn't have a lot of competition.

Nightfall

for Joseph Donahue

If you have no thought in your head
Here's one to think about,

The moment
Of suspended action

When the madwoman
Hears her own cry

And the murderer
Looks in the mirror,

When nothing has happened
Yet it is already too late

To embark on your long-delayed
Study of The Ancient State,

When street passengers
In the hive cities

Of the receding coastlines
Are still trying to get through on their phones—

"If it were different
It wouldn't be difficult"—

Never having imagined
How the voices would persist

Almost past the point
Where there was anyone to listen.

They had woken from apocalypse pop
To find that everything

Had already taken place,
And themselves transported

Beyond the stars they once peered at
In the cold over dark pines,

Woken to find themselves
Weeping in space

Aboard a star ship deviated
Fatally from its course.

The Keyhole

1

What nobody sees
doesn't exist.

2

If nobody spies on it
there can be no scene.

3

The spy is so much part
of the scene spied on

as to be almost without body,
almost without voice or history.

4

The people in the room
exist only in relation

to those eyes that find them out
from a concealed vantage point.

5

Some with a wink or lowered lashes
appear to acknowledge the intrusion.

Without that signal
the spy could not exist,

would stray in the dark
in search of something to look at.

Bedroom Farce

The poor fellow can never quite get
into the bed, or out from under it,

the door being locked
on the outside, and the hallway

crowded with house guests, while she,
as she shimmies down the drainpipe

in a glistening silk negligee, provides proof
to a perpetually eavesdropping in-law

of the thing that might have happened
but never in fact did, and truly

never could have, someone as always
having stumbled into the barn

at precisely the wrong moment,
prompting the supposed "burglar" to jump

from the hayloft by the back window
so as to land in full dinner attire

on an awkwardly placed thornbush,
in time for an overnight visitor

to shriek in surprise Why Jack
what on earth are *you* doing there.

Estrangement

The unseen companion
is a half-heard voice

answering questions
not yet uttered

and shadowing at noon
the bare stone path

to a house
where strangers dwell.

September

"I'm losing it"

you reach for what must have been
at hand a moment ago

a song or TV show
the thing you were going to smoke

"I'm losing it"

the string or button
that held it together

the photographs saved from disappearance
by the one who is disappearing

Epitaph

Knowing myself a target
I failed to keep
a sharp lookout
and when the ambush came
didn't move fast enough.

The Old Tune

"Ashes of love
on a winter day

on a morning
when a dog

feels its age
in an unlit hall"—

A woman who can no longer
make breakfast

without breaking apart
into spasms of mistrust

hears that tune
even on her broken radio.

The Late Crowd

They drift by around midnight
and set the place in an uproar

with their hijinx and bantering,
jokes only the young make,

and not until hours later
do they start to let on

how hard it gets to be
for those without a place

or a name in the icy night,
and a voice the last home left.

The Storm

The wind rages
And we lie in the dark

The cities are tottering
Waves have invaded
The basements of painters
And spoiled all the wine
That the merchants collected

The wind rages
And we lie in the dark

Ferries are sunken
And walking paths drowned
The gate to the terminus
Lies under sand heaps
That let no one enter

The wind rages
And we lie in the dark

Here in the bed
Is a spit of dry land
A big enough hollow

To rest in yet restless
We hold on in silence

The wind rages
With never an ending
And tired beyond telling
We lie in the dark

The Song

Oh faithful travelers
Whither or where you rove

Hold fast the song
I gave you for my love

Let not one syllable
Or breath be forgot

So when you meet her
She may hear each note

Air for the Magicians

in memory of Robert Fagan

1

Out of what corner
of Phrygia do they come

in starry cloaks
and conical hats

approaching with silent steps
what frozen lake,

to compute by ice crystals
the fall of kingdoms

not yet named,
while droning strings

echo the satin
convolutions of robes

that turn like pages
in a book painted by hand?

2

Take away the lush bits
and you end up with gridwork

deeply delighting
in the sustained hum

by which bright emptiness
holds itself together.

3

Each instant
is all of life

whether making slow love
in the thirteenth century

or hunting with mercenaries
for stolen gold

on a mountain road deserted
but for birds of prey—

just that, no more,
a stone oratory

within sound of ocean
glimpsed crossing a cow pasture,

or the parrot's cry
from the vacant apartment

where its owner just died,
or the taste of honeysuckle

under a childhood arbor,
edge of glazed clay

dredged up in noon glare
or surmised range

of an ancient flute part—
the bridge hidden in mist

the guide points out
before he goes—

4
But in whose presence
can I listen as the chord fades

or disentangle
that thicket of inky shadows

making mountain
for monks to sip wine in?

The black splash vibrates
within the scroll,

figures made from rain
shimmer in impenetrable woods.

III

Caller from Ganymede

for Albert Mobilio

1

In the place from which
the signals came
it was already the future
but the future was grown old
and soot-ridden
and stripped of gloss—
In the dusk of the immobilized city
the cars along the river
switched on their headlights
as a bright object fell from space
without one motorist
to see it or cry out—

2

Far from the muffled center
there was an ancient scientist
who in a laboratory equipped
with the latest in obsolete monitors
tracked light-patterns—
assisted by dedicated youngsters,
Jack like a movie star
with glistening curls
and Ann like a secretary
with sculpted hair
who did the typing
even though she was a scientist too
and when the talk turned to the odds
of an incursion from space
was obliged to remind her male colleagues
"I'm an adult!"—

3

This happened long ago
but continues to unfold
as if just coming to pass—
In their lab that resembles
a low-budget recording studio
they work late under globe lamps,
the exhausted Ann brushing off
Jack's occasional half-hearted come-on—
to connect would take too much energy—

4

No suggestion that either
has managed a life
beyond tracking dots in the sky
like the one that plummets
past bridge and tower
into the fields beyond the city
where they find a houseless wasteland
cordoned off by military personnel
checking security clearances,
within a strict perimeter penetrable
only by a top secret double-A rating—

5

Scientists and army men converge
to isolate in sparse grass
between muddied ruts
the intruding presence—
A freezing cold sphere
about the size of a basketball,
of undetermined silicone-like material,
to be boxed and trucked back
to the electronic research center,
dropped on a spare desk
with no more ceremony
than a bundle of dirty laundry—

6

The military are habitually
mistrustful of science,
unable to spell "spectroscope"—
Even as Dr. Morley and his team
communicate among themselves
in secret poetry, their only language—
"A lattice of carbon filaments
containing nothing but a vacuum,
an energy valve of fantastic ingenuity,
a valve which is the slave
of a master system, a thermionic buffer
acting as an automatic monitor
to control the input ratio"—
"Do you mean the transmutation
of matter? Transmitted
from some other planet?"

7

Ann, left alone
to finish the paper work,
picks up frequencies
from the sphere in the next room
and clutches her ballpoint
to ward off the headache
the emanations are giving her,
turning as if toward an escape hatch
to the keyboard of the manual typewriter
and finds in the midst of her agony
that she can no longer type—

8

And here the abyss widens—
The coldness of intergalactic spaces
opens between the tips of her fingers
and the alphabetic grid—
While an amphibious claw-hand
pokes from the storage room
and horror is born
as the orb fabricated
by intelligences light years
in advance of ours
reconstitutes the material form
of a monstrous body
mutated by nuclear weaponry—

9

If the horror did not already
lie in the dilemma
of the secretary who working late
finds herself unable
among stained coffee-cups
and stacks of trade journals
to focus attention
on inventory protocol—
This is the exact moment
where she lost track of her life—

10

Even before Dr. Morley's head exploded
under the influence of wavelengths
our minds cannot tolerate—
The old man was the only one
who knew everything
yet that was not enough
to keep the culture from collapsing
into pockets of envious gossip
and bullying misapprehension—
The old man was the only one
with a proper sense
of fear and awe—

11

Once he has left the scene
a universal degeneracy
afflicts public life,
bureaucrats dither,
newspapers spread panic,
and the police express bafflement
as teenage girls continue to disappear,
one a day, week after week,
because an alien intelligence
has placed an advert
in the back pages of *Bikini Girl*—
"Independent television
and film producer requires talent,
young ladies with looks,
talent and ambition needed,
please write with recent photograph
to box nine six eight"—

12

This is the language
in which the third moon of Jupiter speaks to us—
Mister Medra wears a mask
and sets up shop
in the back room of a porn emporium
disguised as a run-down
second-hand bookstore,
managed by a homosexual pimp
who likes to jive with the vice cops—
"Some people aren't normal, are they?"—
"Some men pay a lot
for a little in my line"—"If you don't
do business with peculiar people
you don't do business in this part of the world"—

13

Past walls hung with back numbers
of *Sir!* and *Cavalcade* and *Black Velvet*
each teenage girl makes her way
to where the doors slide open
and a shadow sits behind a desk—
The dark messenger whose eyes alone
are visible but to whose voice
the girls are drawn irresistibly,
voice of suave command and cultured inflection
ordering each to sit still for her picture
while a steel ball oscillates to vibraphone jazz—

14

Afterwards the photo
is delivered by courier
and the next day she vanishes—
Such a photo as her parents
cannot quite describe—
"Sort of artistic, you know,
it was in color, and I've never
seen one like it before,
one of those new ones,
made of a sort of plastic, in 3-D"—
The latest applicant lies sleepless in bed
and as she stares at her own photo
the eyes stare back at her—
The photo glows
with the remote mind that now inhabits it—
By looking at herself she is looked at—

15

Policemen and scientists
go hunting for lost girls
as night settles on the entertainment district
and moody organ music
plays while taxis glide
through the murky fluid element—
These oblivious spaces—
City of no known language
beyond what is coded
as pin-up shots and police bulletins—

16

The end will come too soon,
Ann will awaken to solitary knowledge,
she will speak to the alien
in a language he understands,
the female scientist having almost
grasped the purport of the universe
climbs, tarted up as a teenage model,
toward the back room, too intent
even to spot the pimp
crumpled dead by the stairway,
past a copy of *Playboy* dangling from a wire,
to ask the fatal question—

17

For this is how remote minds
make contact across infinite distances,
conversing from either side
of a half-empty makeshift book rack—
"I came to see you
to ask you your purpose,
haven't you learned
the futility of violence?"—
And here intelligence having reached its limit
the female scientist
will have to be strangled, but why,
why must Ann be strangled,
she is the only one who understands
how things are, why is she such a threat,
why, why, why does she have to be strangled?—

18

"I fear what I cannot control
and I cannot control an intelligence
almost equal to mine,
we found it impossible
to suppress the emotions
of love and hate,
so we slipped back
into the dark abyss,
there is always someone to fear"—

19

Among rubble from the last war
the angel of intelligence
prepares his departure,
split down the middle,
his face one half trim-bearded beauty
and one half radioactive scar tissue—
On that planet life will be better—
On that planet life will be horror—
The girls having become disembodied
are entered in the sphere—
Their fate lost to us—
On earth now nothing but onlookers
in this city where none
has yet disclosed a place
where we might desire to settle

NOTES

The phrase "blue hill" is a translation of the Swedish "Blåkulla," in Swedish tradition believed to be the gathering place for witches' Sabbaths. In the 1660s several mass trials aimed at those said to have gone there resulted in the public execution of at least 22 people. The poem makes free use of details from Bengt Ankarloo's "Witch Trials in Northern Europe, 1450–1700," included in Ankarloo and Clark, eds., *Witchcraft and Magic in Europe: The Period of the Witch Trials* (Philadelphia: University of Pennsylvania Press, 2002). Ankarloo quotes an eyewitness account of the executions which took place at Mora in August 1669: "They went on Bartholomew's Day, seven on the first pyre, five on the second and three on the third, a horrible spectacle. The pyres were built on a clean and sandy point by the river with water on both sides and in clear and beautiful weather. Several thousand people from all the surrounding parishes were present."

"Caller from Ganymede" is based on the film *The Night Caller* (1965), adapted from Frank Crisp's novel by Jim O'Connolly and directed by John Gilling, and released in the United States as *Blood Beast from Outer Space*. Some dialogue from the film, sometimes in compressed or altered form, has been embedded. The poem was written in response to Albert Mobilio's invitation to participate in the Double Take reading series which he curates at Apexart in New York City.

ACKNOWLEDGMENTS

Some of these poems have appeared in *Battersea Review*, *Projector*, *Southampton Review*, *The Village Voice*, *Hambone*, and *Journal of Poetics Research*. I am grateful to the editors Ben Mazer, Chris Kerr, Star Black, Joshua Mehigan, Nathaniel Mackey, and John Tranter.

TITLES FROM MARSH HAWK PRESS

Jane Augustine, *KRAZY: Visual Poems and Performance Scripts, A Woman's Guide to Mountain Climbing, Night Lights, Arbor Vitae*
Tom Beckett, ~~DIPSTICK~~ *(DIPTYCH)*
Sigman Byrd, *Under the Wanderer's Star*
Patricia Carlin, *Quantum Jitters, Original Green, Second Nature*
Claudia Carlson, *Pocket Park, The Elephant House*
Meredith Cole, *Miniatures*
Jon Curley, Scorch Marks, *Hybrid Moments*
Neil de la Flor, *An Elephant's Memory of Blizzards, Almost Dorothy*
Chard deNiord, *Sharp Golden Thorn*
Sharon Dolin, *Serious Pink*
Steve Fellner, *The Weary World Rejoices, Blind Date with Cavafy*
Thomas Fink, *Selected Poems & Poetic Series, Joyride, Peace Conference, Clarity and Other Poems, After Taxes, Gossip: A Book of Poems*
Norman Finkelstein, *Inside the Ghost Factory, Passing Over*
Edward Foster, *Sewing the Wind, Dire Straits, The Beginning of Sorrows, What He Ought To Know, Mahrem: Things Men Should Do for Men*
Paolo Javier, *The Feeling Is Actual*
Burt Kimmelman, *Somehow, Abandoned Angel*

Burt Kimmelman and Fred Caruso, *The Pond at Cape May Point*
Basil King, *The Spoken Word/the Painted Hand from Learning to Draw/A History 77 Beasts: Basil King's Bestiary, Mirage*
Martha King, *Imperfect Fit*
Phillip Lopate, *At the End of the Day: Selected Poems and An Introductory Essay*
Mary Mackey, *Travelers With No Ticket Home, Sugar Zone, Breaking the Fever*
Jason McCall, *Dear Hero,*
Sandy McIntosh, *Obsessional—Poetry for Performance, A Hole In the Ocean: A Hamptons' Apprenticeship, Cemetery Chess: Selected and New Poems, Ernesta, in the Style of the Flamenco, Forty-Nine Guaranteed Ways to Escape Death, The After-Death History of My Mother, Between Earth and Sky*
Stephen Paul Miller, *Any Lie You Tell Will Be the Truth, There's Only One God and You're Not It, Fort Dad, The Bee Flies in May, Skinny Eighth Avenue*
Daniel Morris, *If Not for the Courage, Bryce Passage, Hit Play*
Sharon Olinka, *The Good City*
Christina Olivares, *No Map of the Earth Includes Stars*
Justin Petropoulos, *Eminent Domain*

Paul Pines, *Gathering Sparks, Divine Madness, Last Call at the Tin Palace, Charlotte Songs*
Jacquelyn Pope, *Watermark*
George Quasha, *Things Done For Themselves*
Karin Randolph, *Either She Was*
Rochelle Ratner, *Ben Casey Days, Balancing Acts, House and Home*
Michael Rerick, *In Ways Impossible to Fold*
Corrine Robins, *Facing It: New and Selected Poems, Today's Menu, One Thousand Years*
Eileen R. Tabios, *The Connoisseur of Alleys, Sun Stigmata, The Thorn Rosary: Selected Prose Poems and New (1998–2010), The Light Sang As It Left Your Eyes: Our Autobiography, I Take Thee, English, for My Beloved, Reproductions of the Empty Flagpole*
Eileen R. Tabios and j/j hastain, *the relational elations of ORPHANED ALGEBRA*
Susan Terris, *Ghost of Yesterday, Natural Defenses*
Madeline Tiger, *Birds of Sorrow and Joy*
Tana Jean Welch, *Latest Volcano*
Harriet Zinnes, *New and Selected Poems, Weather Is Whether, Light Light or the Curvature of the Earth, Whither Nonstopping, Drawing on the Wall*

YEAR	AUTHOR	MHP POETRY PRIZE TITLE	JUDGE
2004	Jacquelyn Pope	*Watermark*	Marie Ponsot
2005	Sigman Byrd	*Under the Wanderer's Star*	Gerald Stern
2006	Steve Fellner	*Blind Date With Cavafy*	Denise Duhamel
2007	Karin Randolph	*Either She Was*	David Shapiro
2008	Michael Rerick	*In Ways Impossible to Fold*	Thylias Moss
2009	Neil de la Flor	*Almost Dorothy*	Forrest Gander
2010	Justin Petropoulos	*Eminent Domain*	Anne Waldman
2011	Meredith Cole	*Miniatures*	Alicia Ostriker
2012	Jason McCall	*Dear Hero,*	Cornelius Eady
2013	Tom Beckett	~~DIPSTICK~~ *(DIPTYCH)*	Charles Bernstein
2014	Christina Olivares	*No Map of the Earth Includes Stars*	Brenda Hillman
2015	Tana Jean Welch	*Latest Volcano*	Stephanie Strickland
2016	Robert Gibb	*After*	Mark Doty
2017	Geoffrey O'Brien	*The Blue Hill*	Meena Alexander

ARTISTIC ADVISORY BOARD

Toi Derricotte, Denise Duhamel, Marilyn Hacker, Allan Kornblum *(in memorium)*, Maria Mazzioti Gillan, Alicia Ostriker, Marie Ponsot, David Shapiro, Nathaniel Tarn, Anne Waldman, and John Yau.